Rock Music Library

John Lennon

by June Preszler

Consultant: Meredith Rutledge
Assistant Curator
Rock and Roll Hall of Fame and Museum
Cleveland, Ohio

Mankato, Minnesota

GRASSLAND MIDDLE LIBRARY MC

Edge Books are published by Capstone Press
151 Good Counsel Drive, P.O. Box 669, Mankato, Minnesota 56002
www.capstonepress.com

Copyright © 2005 by Capstone Press. All rights reserved.
No part of this publication may be reproduced in whole or in part, or stored in a retrieval system, or transmitted in any form or by any means, electronic, mechanical, photocopying, recording, or otherwise, without written permission of the publisher.
For information regarding permission, write to Capstone Press,
151 Good Counsel Drive, P.O. Box 669, Dept. R, Mankato, Minnesota 56002.
Printed in the United States of America

Library of Congress Cataloging-in-Publication Data
Preszler, June, 1954–
   John Lennon / by June Preszler.
   p. cm.—(Edge Books. Rock music library)
   Includes bibliographical references and index.
   ISBN 0-7368-2701-3 (hardcover)
   1. Lennon, John, 1940–1980—Juvenile literature. 2. Rock musicians—Biography—Juvenile literature. [1. Lennon, John, 1940–1980. 2. Musicians. 3. Rock music.]
I. Title. II. Series.
ML3930.L34P74 2005
782.42166'092—dc22   2003026403

Summary: Traces the life, career, and lasting impact of rock music legend John Lennon.

Editorial Credits
Angela Kaelberer, editor; Jason Knudson, series designer; Molly Nei, book designer; Jo Miller, photo researcher; Scott Thoms, photo editor; Eric Kudalis, product planning editor

Photo Credits
Corbis/Bettmann, 11, 25; Hulton-Deutsch Collection, 12, 18; Lynn Goldsmith, 23; Reuters NewMedia Inc., 27; S.I.N./Kim Tonelli, 29; Susan Phillips, 22
Getty Images Inc./Hulton Archive, cover, 5, 10, 15, 17; Pictorial Press, 9; Time Life Pictures/David McGough, 6
Globe Photos Inc., 21

1 2 3 4 5 6 09 08 07 06 05 04

Table of Contents

Chapter 1:
Rock and Roll — 4

Chapter 2:
A Young Talent — 8

Chapter 3:
The Beatles and Beyond — 16

Chapter 4:
John's Influence — 24

Oasis — 29

Glossary — 30

Read More — 31

Internet Sites — 31

Index — 32

CHAPTER 1

Rock and Roll

In 1955 in Liverpool, England, John Lennon tuned his radio to Radio Luxembourg. John listened as Elvis Presley's new song, "Heartbreak Hotel," blared from the radio. The focus of John's world changed.

The music of Elvis, Chuck Berry, and Little Richard gave 15-year-old John a new direction. John said once he heard rock and roll, he knew his future would include music.

Learn about:

Music lover

First band

A lasting influence

Rock and roll music changed John Lennon's life.

John recorded several albums with his wife, Yoko Ono.

The Quarry Men

John felt power in rock and roll. By 1957, he and several friends had formed the Quarry Men. The band was named after their high school, the Quarry Bank Grammar School.

The Quarry Men often played for free. John didn't care about being paid. John's aunt Mimi, who raised him, didn't approve of his interest in music. Mimi thought John would never be able to make a living in a band.

A Musical Legend

John proved Mimi wrong. He started the Beatles, which became the world's most popular rock band. When the group broke up, John continued his musical career with his wife, Yoko Ono. John and Yoko also worked for world peace.

John died in 1980, but his work still influences songwriters. In 1990, *Time* magazine named John one of the 10 most important people of the 20th century. He was the only entertainer on the list.

CHAPTER 2

A Young Talent

In 1938, John's mother, Julia Stanley, married Alfred Lennon against her family's wishes. Alfred worked on ships. He was at sea when John was born October 9, 1940.

About 1945, Alfred and Julia separated. Julia's sister Mimi thought she could give John a better home. Mimi talked Julia into letting John live with Mimi and her husband, George Smith.

Julia lived near Mimi and George, but John seldom saw her until he was about 14. At that time, Julia and John became close. Julia introduced John to music and taught him to play the banjo.

Learn about:

- Childhood
- Breaking into music
- Beatlemania

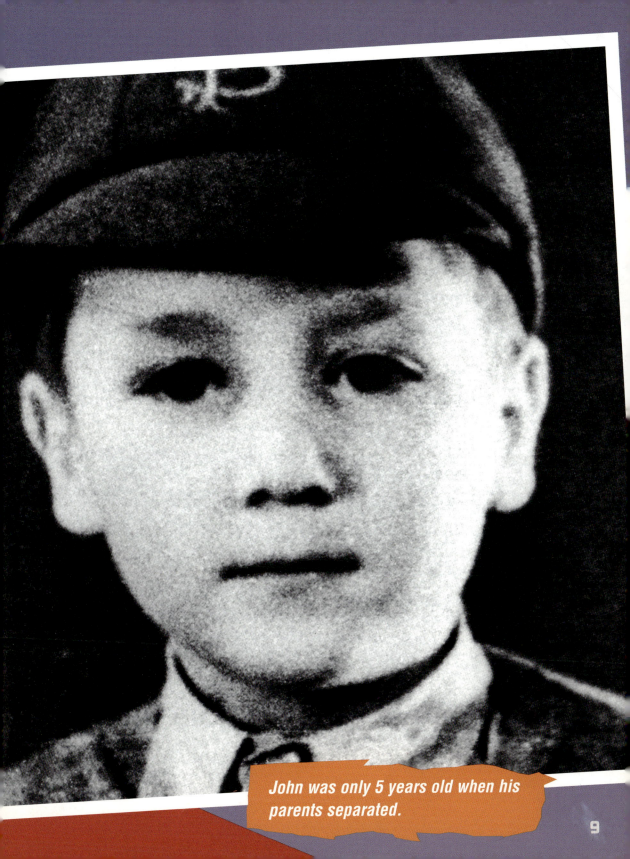

John was only 5 years old when his parents separated.

John continued to be close to his mother until she died in 1958. After Julia's death, music became even more important to John.

Musical Beginnings

In 1957, John met Paul McCartney when the Quarry Men played at a church social. Paul soon joined the band.

By the end of the 1950s, the Quarry Men were playing at the Cavern and other jazz

By 1962, the Quarry Men had become the Beatles.

Paul McCartney (left) and John wrote most of the Beatles' songs.

clubs in Liverpool. One music lover, George Harrison, begged to join the group. George was younger than the other band members. But he was so talented that John let him join.

In 1960, the band changed its name to the Silver Beetles. Later, John changed the spelling of Beetles to include the word "beat." The band then dropped Silver and became the Beatles.

John and Cynthia married in 1962.

John, Paul, George, and Ringo

By early 1962, the Beatles had a contract with a manager named Brian Epstein. They recorded a demo tape. Epstein took the tape to the major record companies in London. Each company turned him down. The Beatles didn't give up. They kept playing and writing songs. They had big plans and dreams.

Later that year, those dreams began to come true. Producer George Martin offered to record the band's first album. But Martin didn't like the band's drummer, Pete Best. Ringo Starr replaced Pete.

John's personal life was changing as fast as his professional life. In August 1962, John married Cynthia Powell. Their son, Julian, was born April 8, 1963.

Beatles in America

In late December 1963, the Beatles' record company released "I Want to Hold Your Hand" in the United States. Epstein booked the Beatles on *The Ed Sullivan Show*, a popular TV program.

When the Beatles performed on the show in February 1964, they were already popular with U.S. teenagers. Both "I Want to Hold Your Hand" and "She Loves You" were worldwide hits. Beatlemania had begun.

Edge Fact
About 73 million Americans watched the Beatles' first appearance on *The Ed Sullivan Show*. At the time, the audience was the largest ever for a TV show.

On February 9, 1964, the Beatles performed on The Ed Sullivan Show.

CHAPTER 3

The Beatles and Beyond

The next two years brought unbelievable success to the Beatles. The band had many hit songs and sold millions of records. They were the most popular rock band in the world.

The band members didn't always handle their success well. By late 1966, all four Beatles used illegal drugs. John and George often used LSD.

The use of drugs wasn't the only change in John's life. In 1966, he met artist Yoko Ono at a London art gallery. John and Yoko fell in love. John and Cynthia divorced in 1968. In 1969, John and Yoko married.

Learn about:

- The end of the Beatles
- Back to music
- Tragedy in New York City

In 1967, the Beatles were on top of the music world.

In 1969, John and Yoko had a "bed-in" demonstration for peace.

A New Path

John and Yoko were active in the peace movement. They were against the Vietnam War (1954–1975). John's songs "Give Peace a Chance" and "Imagine" became songs for the peace movement.

John and Yoko also began making music together. They started the Plastic Ono Band. By late 1969, John decided to leave the Beatles. The group broke up in 1970.

A Difficult Time

The early 1970s were hard years for John. His use of drugs and alcohol caused problems in his marriage. In 1973, John and Yoko separated. John moved to Los Angeles. Yoko lived in New York City.

John returned to New York City in 1974. In early 1975, he and Yoko got back together. Soon, John and Yoko were expecting a baby. John was happy about the news. He hadn't spent much time with his first child, Julian. John wanted to have a better relationship with his new child.

Staying Home

On October 9, 1975, Yoko and John's son, Sean, was born. The day was John's 35th birthday. For the next five years, John took care of Sean while Yoko worked on the family's business interests.

Early in 1980, both John and Yoko returned to music. In November 1980, their *Double Fantasy* album was released. The album was instantly popular. John was ready for a comeback.

"People are always judging you, or criticizing what you're trying to say on one little album, on one little song, but to me it's a lifetime's work. From the boyhood paintings and poetry to when I die—it's all part of one big production ... to me, my work is one piece."—John Lennon, December 5, 1980

John spent as much time as possible with Yoko and Sean.

The Ending

On December 8, 1980, John and Yoko returned to their apartment near Central Park in New York City. They had finished a recording session for Yoko's new song. As they stepped out of their car, they heard a voice call, "Mr. Lennon." As John turned his head, a man shot him five times in the back. John died from his wounds.

Fans outside John's apartment building mourned John's death.

Fans all over the world expressed their feelings for John after his death.

Later that night, Yoko sent a short message to John's fans. She told them that John loved and prayed for everyone. She asked his fans to do the same for him.

Chapter 4

John's Influence

Word of John's death spread quickly. Fans stood outside his boyhood home in Liverpool. They brought flowers, banners, pictures, and candles. In New York's Central Park, about 400,000 people honored John.

Fans showed their sadness and respect in many ways. About 250,000 letters of sympathy arrived at John and Yoko's home. At least 7 million copies of *Double Fantasy* sold within the next several months. In 1984, New York City set aside a small section of Central Park in John's honor. The city named the area Strawberry Fields after a Beatles song.

Learn about:

Sorrow for John

Tributes

John's music today

Sean, Yoko, and Julian (front row, left to right) attended the dedication of Strawberry Fields in 1984.

John's influence continues today. Musicians around the world record the songs he wrote and sang. "Give Peace a Chance" and "Imagine" were played following the September 11, 2001, terrorist attacks in New York City.

TV Event

On October 9, 2001, a TV event featured John's music. *Come Together: A Night for John Lennon's Words and Music* became a concert of prayer and healing for New York City. The concert featured John's songs performed by

Edge Fact
The man who killed John was tried and sent to prison. Some people believe that printing the killer's name gives him too much attention. Fans want to remember how John lived, not who killed him.

Sean Lennon sang John's song "Julia" at the concert honoring John's music.

today's musicians. Performers included Moby, Dave Matthews, the Stone Temple Pilots, Nelly Furtado, and Marc Anthony. John's son Sean also performed at the concert.

Remembering John

John Lennon is remembered for more than his music. John combined artistic ability, musical genius, and seriousness that went beyond pop music. He was an artist, an author, and a poet. At the New York City concert, the last song was "Give Peace a Chance." This song reminded people that John was also a man who dreamed of a more peaceful world.

"The idea of peace has always been with us … it's like the Beatles singing 'All You Need Is Love'—I'm just singing 'All You Need Is Peace' now."
—John Lennon, 1969

Oasis

Brothers Liam and Noel Gallagher formed Oasis in 1991. The band's hit songs include "Live Forever," "Supersonic," and "Wonderwall."

Oasis band members say they learned much about music from the Beatles, especially John Lennon. Noel Gallagher says he compares every song he writes to the work of the Beatles. Some of the band's songs include quotes by the Beatles. "Don't Look Back in Anger" includes a reference to John's peace demonstrations, "So, I'll start the revolution from my bed."

Glossary

comeback (KUHM-bak)—a return to a former position; at the time of his death, John Lennon was about to make a comeback in the music world.

influence (IN-floo-uhnss)—to have an effect on someone or something

peace movement (PEESS MOOVE-muhnt)—efforts made by a group of people to stop wars

revolution (rev-uh-LOO-shun)—an uprising by a group of people against a system of government or a way of life

terrorist (TER-ur-ist)—a person who uses violence or threats to get something from a group of people or government

Read More

Gogerly, Liz. *John Lennon: Voice of a Generation.* Famous Lives. Austin, Texas: Raintree Steck-Vaughn, 2003.

Kallen, Stuart A. *John Lennon.* The Importance of. San Diego: Lucent, 2002.

White, Michael. *John Lennon.* World Musicmakers. San Diego: Blackbirch Press, 2004.

Internet Sites

FactHound offers a safe, fun way to find Internet sites related to this book. All of the sites on FactHound have been researched by our staff.

Here's how:
1. Visit *www.facthound.com*
2. Type in this special code **0736827013** for age-appropriate sites. Or enter a search word related to this book for a more general search.
3. Click on the **Fetch It** button.

FactHound will fetch the best sites for you!

Index

Beatles, 7, 11, 13, 14, 16, 19, 24, 29
Best, Pete, 13
birth, 8

death, 7, 22–23, 24
Double Fantasy, 20, 24
drug use, 16, 19

Ed Sullivan Show, The, 14
Epstein, Brian, 13, 14

Harrison, George, 11, 16

Lennon, Alfred (father), 8
Lennon, Cynthia Powell, 13, 16
Lennon, Julia (mother), 8, 10
Lennon, Julian (son), 13, 19
Lennon, Sean (son), 20, 27
Liverpool, England, 4, 11, 24

Martin, George, 13
McCartney, Paul, 10

New York City, 19, 22, 24, 26, 28

Oasis, 29
Ono, Yoko, 7, 16, 19, 20, 22–23, 24

peace movement, 7, 19, 28, 29
Plastic Ono Band, 19

Quarry Men, 7, 10–11

Smith, Mimi (aunt), 7, 8
songs, 4, 7, 13, 14, 16, 19, 22, 24, 26–28, 29
Starr, Ringo, 13
Strawberry Fields, 24

tributes, 7, 24, 26–28

GRASSLAND MIDDLE LIBRARY MC

333753